# BLACK'S PICTURE INFORMATION BOOKS

**Scientific Adviser Jean Imrie MSc**

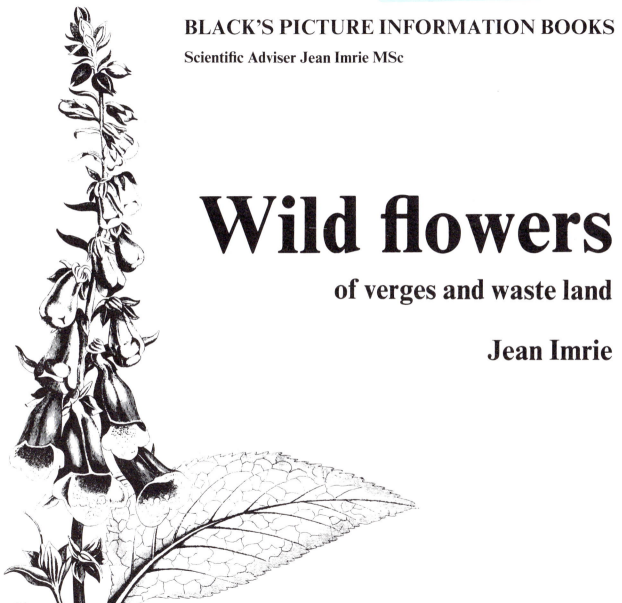

# Wild flowers

## of verges and waste land

**Jean Imrie**

**Adam and Charles Black · London**

Published by A & C Black Ltd
35 Bedford Row, London WC1R 4JH
First published 1977
© 1977 A & C Black Ltd
ISBNs 0 7136 1696 2 (cased)
       0 7136 1697 0 (paper)

Filmset by Keyspools Limited, Golborne, Lancs.
Printed in Great Britain by Tindal Press, Chelmsford

## Acknowledgements

The colour photographs are reproduced by kind permission of:
A–Z Botanical Collections cover, 1, 2, 3, 4, 6, 7, 8, 10, 11, 12, 13, 14, 16, 18, 19, 21, 23, 24, 25, 26, 27, 29, 30, 31, 32, 33, 35, 36, 37, 40, 44, 45, 46, 49, 50, 51, 52, 56, 57, 58, 60, 61, 62, 63, 64, 65, 66, 67, 68;
Aquila Photographics 28;
Ardea: I R Beames 47, S Gooders 42, J L Mason 17, P Morris 9;
Bob Baines 53, 55;
J P Imrie 34, 38, 41, 43, 48, 70, 71;
Mrs C Johnson 5, 15, 20, 22, 39, 69

The black and white photographs are reproduced by kind permission of:
A–Z Botanical Collections pages 11, 42, 43, 47;
Press Agency York 41;
R Price 8a, 9, 46;
John Topham Picture Library 6, 7, 8b;
P F White 48.

The drawings on pages 12, 13, 14, 15, 44, 45 are by Vanessa Luff.

# Contents

*Broom*

*A mass of flowers beside a quiet country road*

# The habitats

Flowering plants grow in all kinds of places and you can find plants in flower in every month of the year. You don't have to go far afield to find a great variety of colour and shape in flowers and to gather a few of them to look at and to name.

The easiest way is to walk along a quiet country lane looking at everything growing at the sides, or to look carefully at a neglected area of a town or village. Roadside verges and waste land provide many different plants for you to study. You will find big changes in the plants as spring passes into summer, then into autumn and winter, so it is worth taking the same walk, or visiting the same place several times in one year.

Roadside verges vary a good deal from one part of the country to another. In some places the sides of the roads rise steeply to form banks and these may be overgrown with a variety of plants. Or, where a road passes through a cutting, the sides may be almost bare rock where only a few plants can find a foothold. In other parts of the country, stone walls take the place of hedges and a few plants manage to grow in the soil which is blown into the cracks and crevices. Elsewhere, the road may have ditches on one or both sides, and plants which like damp ground will grow there.

Motorways and main roads everywhere have wide margins and central reservations where many flowers flourish. Cars and buses are not allowed to stop on these highways, so you have to recognise the flowers at a distance! But country lanes are good places to find flowers

and when you become familiar with the plants growing there, you will recognise the motorway plants as you speed by.

*Pennywort* Umbilicus rupestris *growing in the cracks of a roadside stone wall*

Perhaps you cannot think of any waste land close to your home, but take a very careful look next time you are out and you will be surprised how much there is. In towns there are often empty sites, waiting for buildings to be erected. Old buildings are often pulled down many months, even years, before new ones are put in their place and these derelict sites are very soon invaded by plants of all kinds. Sometimes old houses in city streets are boarded up before being pulled down, and the neglected doorways provide enough shelter and blown dust to support a variety of plants. Sites awaiting development into new housing estates are temporary 'waste' land. When drains are dug for the houses and the roads, the existing plants are disturbed and the soil is often left in heaps. These soil heaps are rapidly covered with new plants.

*Coltsfoot growing among the rubbish in a car dump*

*You can find wild flowers flourishing alongside industrial sites*

Some towns are built close to rivers or streams: where the banks are too steep for building, the land is neglected. Sometimes these banks are used for tipping rubbish and the edges of tips and dumps often support many different plants. Road-widening and road-straightening schemes may leave quite large areas of rough land, and motorway construction often creates patches of bare earth. If these are left undisturbed for any length of time they are invaded by plants.

Railway stations (especially beyond the platforms), old sidings and, best of all, disused railway lines, even in the middle of towns, provide plenty of flowers to study. Stone, slate and limestone quarries also create 'waste' areas; once the useful stone has been extracted, the whole quarry is often simply abandoned. On a quarry floor, especially in a limestone area, you can find a variety of species not often found elsewhere.

*Even in winter there are plants growing along this disused railway line*

# The plants

*Hemlock* Conium maculatum

Naming plants is not as easy as it sounds. You probably know the lesser celandine (picture 20) which is one of the first flowers to open in early spring. Some people call it pilewort, others call it golden guineas or butter and cheese. The cuckoo-pint (28 & 29) is less common, but it is also known as wild arum, lords and ladies, parson-in-the-pulpit and several other names. It can be very confusing indeed when one flower has several names in different parts of one country and of course botanists from different countries describe their flowers in their own language. The dandelion (18) in French is *piss-en-lit* (it is said to have a value as a medicine), in German it is *Lowenzahn* and in Spanish *amar-gon*.

Fortunately for us all, a Swedish naturalist, Carl Linnaeus, made things much simpler. He lived from 1707 to 1778. He gave every known plant a Latin name of two words only. The first word is the **genus** to which the plant belongs (rather like a surname). The second word is the name of the **species** (or forename). So all over the world the lesser celandine is known as *Ranunculus ficaria*, the cuckoo-pint as *Arum maculatum* and the dandelion as *Taraxacum officinale*.

This book describes some of the commonest plants you are likely to find growing in these places. Perhaps you know some of the names already, but it will help you to name others. Look for the fruits and seeds of the flowers you know and try to think why they are growing there and how they arrived. Were they always there? Are they spreading?

Nobody wants the common names of our flowers to be forgotten, and they will always be used in every-day conversation. But if we want to be quite certain that everybody has the same plant in mind, we must use the Latin name as well. Many new plants have been found since Linnaeus died, but his method of naming them is still used.

# Families

There are about 2100 different named wild flowers in this country and these are grouped into families. The largest family is the Compositae, to which the coltsfoot (15), butterbur (17), daisy (47), groundsel (36), ragworts (37 & 38) and thistle (39) belong. Greater stitchwort (22) and red campion (23) both belong to the Caryophyllaceae family. Cow parsley (26) and sweet cicely (27), hogweed (42) and ground elder (59) all belong to the Umbelliferae family.

Each family contains a number of genera (which is the plural of genus) and often many species. Because there are some tiny differences even within a species, botanists may divide the species into a number of **sub-specics** or **varieties**. There are said to be a hundred varieties of dandelion, and four hundred different varieties of blackberry have been described. Very few people can recognise all of these.

*Dog rose*

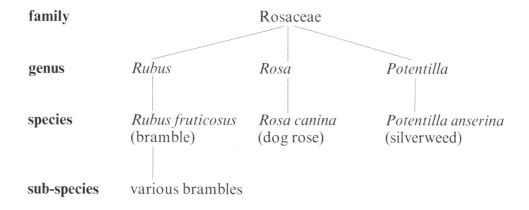

| **family** | Rosaceae | | |
|---|---|---|---|
| **genus** | *Rubus* | *Rosa* | *Potentilla* |
| **species** | *Rubus fruticosus* (bramble) | *Rosa canina* (dog rose) | *Potentilla anserina* (silverweed) |
| **sub-species** | various brambles | | |

# Identifying the plants

How do you start to put the flowering plants into their families? It isn't easy to see why the daisy (47), dandelion (18) and thistle (39) belong to the same family. Nor is it obvious at first why the greater stitchwort (22) and the red campion (23) belong to another family. But as you look more closely at a number of plants, you will find similarities which you could easily miss at first glance.

It is not only the colour of the petals which is important. Look at the shape and size of the leaves and see if they form a rosette on the ground. Are there any leaves on the flower stalk? If you cut across the stem, is it round, square or triangular? Is the plant hairy or smooth? Where is the plant growing?

Flowers are arranged on the stem in a variety of ways: sometimes there is only one, as in the silverweed (51), but more often there are several. These are rarely all open at the same time. Some of the different arrangements are shown below.

It is not important to remember all these names, but it is important to notice the variety.

It is easy to think of the plantain or the cuckoo-pint or the daisy as a single flower, but in fact each is really an **inflorescence** made up of a large number of tiny flowers called **florets**. Can you see now one similarity between the dandelion, the daisy and the thistle? They all have heads of tiny florets packed closely together.

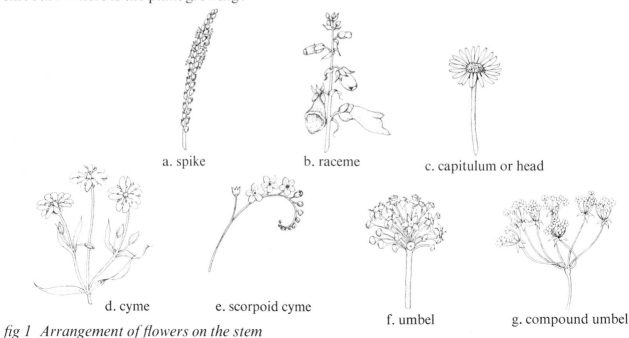

a. spike　　　b. raceme　　　c. capitulum or head

d. cyme　　　e. scorpoid cyme　　　f. umbel　　　g. compound umbel

*fig 1　Arrangement of flowers on the stem*

# Flowers

Most of our flowers have four distinct parts: the **sepals** (which together form the **calyx**), the **petals** (which together form the **corolla**), the **stamens** and the **pistil**. A flower with all four parts is said to be a **complete** flower. The primrose is an example of a complete flower of this kind.

If you look closely at a number of flowers growing on verges and waste land, you will find that there are some similarities but also many differences from this pattern. For instance, bluebells (fig 2, below) and ramsons (25) do not have distinct sepals and petals, but instead they have six petals; three outer ones and three inner ones, each separate from the other and not forming a tube. They have six stamens and one pistil.

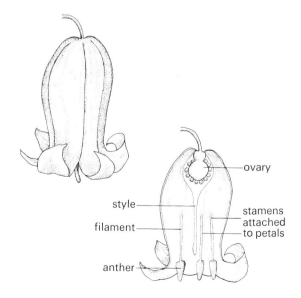

*fig 2 Bluebell*

If you pull apart a dandelion head and use a lens to examine a single floret, you will see that the calyx of each is made up of a ring of hairs and is not leafy as in the primrose. In this case the five petals are joined together to form a strap-like corolla.

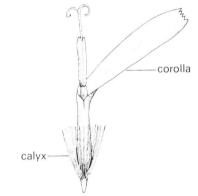

*fig 3 Dandelion floret*

More interesting still, the daisy has two distinct kinds of floret. The ones in the centre have no sepals, but each has a tiny corolla, five stamens and a tiny pistil. These are called **disc florets**. The white, strap-shaped outer florets have no stamens and are called **ray florets**.

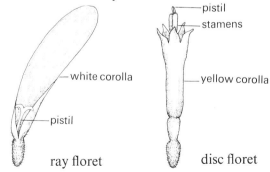

*fig 4 Daisy florets*

There is great variety among flowering plants in the shape of the petals, their colour and their arrangement in the flower. There is variety too in the number and shape of the stamens, ranging from only two in the speedwells to many in the buttercup and the rose. The pistil in the primrose shows three distinct areas: the stigma at the top, looking like a tiny knob, the thin stem or style and the rounded ovary at the base. Some examples of pistils are illustrated below.

In some cases, the stamens are found in some flowers and the pistils in quite separate ones. In the red campion *Silene dioica* (23), all the flowers have five pink or red indented petals and all look alike. Closer inspection shows that some have ten large stamens and a very tiny pistil which does not develop. Others have a well-developed pistil with five styles and only a ring of small knobs instead of stamens. Such flowers are unisexual.

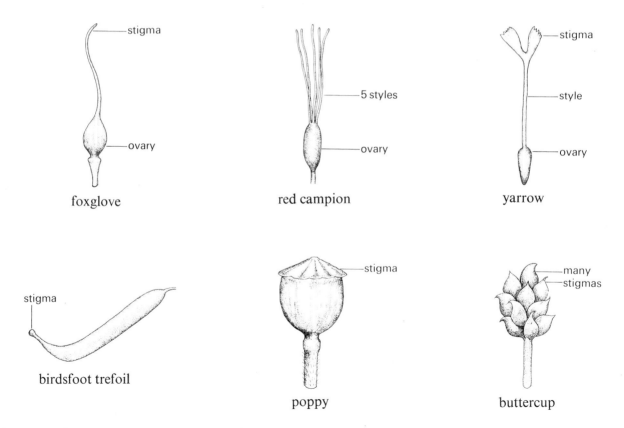

fig 5  Pistils

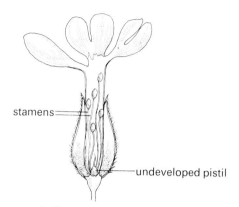

stamens

undeveloped pistil

male flower — ten stamens

In the red campion, only male flowers are found on one plant and female flowers on a quite distinct and separate plant.

The cuckoo-pint *Arum maculatum* is different. The inflorescence is really a spike of tiny florets formed inside the big green sheath. There are no petals or sepals at all.

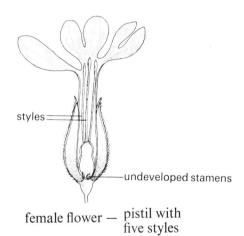

styles

undeveloped stamens

female flower — pistil with five styles

*fig 6  Red campion*

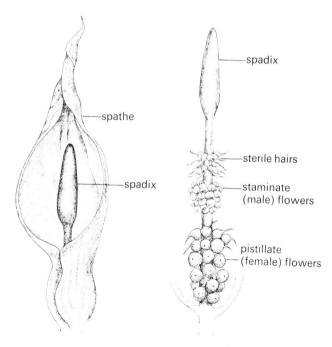

spathe

spadix

spadix

sterile hairs

staminate (male) flowers

pistillate (female) flowers

*fig 7  Cuckoo-pint*

The flowers with stamens are called male flowers, sometimes shown by the symbol ♂. The flowers with pistils are called female flowers, shown by the symbol ♀. When a flower has both stamens and pistils it is called hermaphrodite, ☿.

These features are important in deciding which plants can be grouped into one family. Once this has been done, similarities and differences are used to sort the plants into different genera. It is the smaller but still quite clear differences between the plants in each genus which separate them into individual species, each with its own name.

Sometimes it is easy to recognise a plant and to name it correctly: for example, a dandelion is *Taraxacum offinale*. But there are many plants with flowers which resemble the dandelion, such as hawkweed, or hawkbit, or goatsbeard, and it takes practice to know which is which.

Similarly, the flowers of cow parsley (26), sweet cicely (27), hogweed (42) and ground elder (59) look very much alike and only small differences show that they are separate plants. But sweet cicely smells of aniseed when you crush it, and the leaves of hogweed are much coarser than those of cow parsley and sweet cicely. Hogweed is in flower later in the year too, so you are unlikely to find it at the same time as the others.

**The pictures and descriptions**

The illustrations on pages 17–39 will help you to name many of the common plants which you can find at the roadside or in the waste land close to your home. Illustrations 1–5 show the woody plants which occur most frequently as hedge plants beside roads and between fields. Some of these are planted to provide a thick and prickly barrier which will keep cows and sheep from straying on to the road. They also help keep out trespassers.

Illustrations 6–14 show some of the plants which use the hedge as a support and which make their way through the branches to obtain as much light and air as they can.

The herbaceous plants illustrated in numbers 15–56 can all be found by the roadside. The first ones come into flower in the early months of the year, the later ones in the late spring through to the summer months and into the early autumn.

Illustrations 57–68 show plants which are found mainly on waste ground, but they are sometimes found on roadside verges too. Look out for them everywhere, for they are quite common, though they are sometimes overlooked because they do not always have very showy flowers.

## 1. Blackthorn *Prunus spinosa*

The small white flowers of the blackthorn appear on the black twigs in March and April, before the leaves unfold. The flowers produce nectar and are visited by small flies with a long proboscis and by butterflies and wasps. The fruits look like small damsons and are called sloes. Country people often use them to make sloe gin.

1

## 2. Hawthorn
*Crataegus monogyna*

Most people can recognise the white blossom of this very common hedge plant. The blossom appears in May and is commonly called 'May'. The flowers have a very strong scent and they produce nectar which attracts many species of flies. The fruits ripen to a bright red colour and are an important source of winter food for many birds. They can also be used in jelly and wine making.

2

3

4

**3. Elder** *Sambucus nigra*

The leaves show green early in the spring and the cream-coloured flowers later develop into shiny black berries, often used to make syrups and wines.

**4. Dog rose** *Rosa canina*

There are many different species of wild rose but this is the commonest one. The plant clambers amongst the hedge plants and uses its prickles for anchorage.

**5. Blackberry** *Rubus fruticosus*

The blackberry is another plant which, like the wild rose, makes its way through the stiffer hedge plants. There are many varieties,

5

commonly known as brambles, with white or pink flowers, and all produce juicy black fruits when ripe in late summer.

### 6. Traveller's joy
*Clematis vitalba*

This plant is sometimes called old man's beard from the mass of feathery fruits which are shown here. The small greenish-yellow flowers, seen in summer, have four petals. The plant climbs by twisting its long leaf stalks around any support it can find, and it sometimes reaches the top of quite tall trees. It is most common on chalky soils.

### 7. Honeysuckle
*Lonicera periclymenum*

The stems twine around any support available and the leaves can be seen very early in the year. The long, tubular, sweet-scented flowers are visited by moths and butterflies and produce red berries in the autumn.

### 8. Woody nightshade
*Solanum dulcamara*

Sometimes called bittersweet, this plant scrambles over the rest of the vegetation. It has conspicuous purple flowers and the exposed stamens make a yellow cone in the centre. The flowers produce poisonous egg-shaped berries, green at first, becoming yellow and finally red.

6

7

8

9

10

11

### 9. Ivy *Hedera helix*

The illustration shows the ivy climbing up a tree trunk. It is an evergreen plant and the stem produces side roots which help to fasten the plant on to its support. Its small greenish flowers open very late in the year, September to November, and develop into black berries which are eaten by birds.

### 10. Black bryony
*Tamus communis*

The green stems twine in a clockwise direction and use any available support. They produce spikes of small yellowish-green flowers but these are not as easily seen as the poisonous red berries shown here. There are separate male and female plants, but many more male than female, all visited by insects for nectar.

### 11. White bryony *Bryonia dioica*

This is unrelated to the previous plant. It develops special spring-like growths called tendrils which twist round the support plants. Its leaves are quite different from the black bryony but the flowers are similar, though larger. They are uni-sexual and are visited by many insects, including bees. The female flowers produce pois-onous red berries.

12

13

14

## 12. Larger bindweed or bellbine
*Calystegia sepium*

This is a most troublesome weed if it gets into the garden, for its roots and underground stems go very deep. It is also known as large bindweed, woodbine, bear-bine, ropewind, hellweed and devil's vine, names which show its habit.

Large white or pink flowers grow at odd intervals on the climbing stems. The leaves are large and these, together with the vigorous anti-clockwise growth of the stem, sometimes destroy the hedge plants up which it climbs.

## 13. Bindweed
*Convolvulus arvensis*

This is another plant which can be a nuisance to the gardener. The root system may spread over as much as 30 square metres in a single season and its vertical roots may reach to a depth of 4·5 metres. The trumpet-shaped flowers open in the early morning and close soon after dark and in cold and damp weather. They are visited by insects for nectar and it has been estimated that one plant may produce 600 seeds in a year.

## 14. Goosegrass *Galium aparine*

The stems of this scrambling plant may reach a height of 1·5 m where there are plenty of sup-porting twigs. It clings by means of small curved prickles which run down the four angles of the stem. The tiny white flowers have four petals and produce small green fruits covered with hooked bristles. These cling to animals and to clothing which brushes past them, and the fruits are carried to new places where they can grow.

15

16

18

17

### 15 & 16. Coltsfoot
*Tussilago farfara*

This is one of the first plants to flower in the spring. The bright yellow flower heads can be seen long before the leaves. Illustration 16 shows the disc florets in the centre, surrounded by the narrow tubular ray florets. There may be up to 40 disc florets, all ♂, and up to 300 ray florets, all ♀. The entire head closes up at night. When the flowers have been pollinated, the head droops downward, becoming erect again when the fruits are ripe for dispersal. Each fruit has a parachute of white hairs.

### 17. Butterbur *Petasites hybridus*

Each flowering stalk bears 6–18 spikes of pale pink flower heads which appear in March, before the huge leaves. Each plant has either male or female flowers, but never both. The fruits look like a number of small dandelion 'clocks' on a single stalk.

## 18. Common dandelion
*Taraxacum officinale*

Most people know this plant by sight, but few look at the flower closely. Each head has an average of a hundred and eighty florets, all with stamens and a pistil. Strangely, the dandelion does not need to be fertilised in order to produce fruits. Each fruit has the familiar 'parachute' for dispersal by wind.

## 19. Dog's mercury
*Mercurialis perennis*

You may have to look carefully to see the flowers because the plant is so leafy that they are often hidden. They are small and greenish in colour, and are found in little hanging spikes at the base of the leaves. The plant has either male or female flowers, never both. It can cover a large area of ground and is especially common in limestone districts.

## 20. Lesser celandine
*Ranunculus ficaria*

These bright yellow flowers appear in early spring. They belong to the same genus as the buttercups of our meadows, but

**19**

**20**

**21**

they have a shorter flower stalk, each bearing only one flower. Each flower has usually three sepals and 8–12 golden yellow petals which fade to white. The flowers are visited by insects but few fruits develop. The plant produces tiny bulbils in the axils between the leaves and the stem. These bulbils grow into new plants. It also forms root tubers which make new plants.

## 21. Jack-by-the-hedge or garlic mustard *Alliaria petiolata*

This is a very common plant by the roadside. The name garlic mustard refers to the smell of garlic when the leaves are crushed. The flowers are only about 6 mm across but they are visited by a number of hoverflies and other insects. In spite of this, the flowers are always self-pollinated.

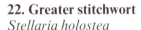

22

23

24

## 22. Greater stitchwort
*Stellaria holostea*

The large white flowers look as though they have ten petals. In fact they have five petals with a deep cleft in the centre of each. There are ten stamens and a pistil with three styles. The flowers are visited by many flies, small bees and beetles.

## 23. Red campion *Lychnis dioica*

This is a tall plant, up to 90 cm in height, and bears bright red flowers from May onwards. Some plants produce the male flowers, each with ten stamens, and others have the female flowers only, each containing a single pistil with five hair-like styles. The flowers are visited by bumble bees and hoverflies.

## 24. Herb robert
*Geranium robertianum*

This plant can be found in flower from April to November. It has clear pink flowers, 1–2 cm across, and fern-like leaves. The leaves often turn red in the autumn. Each flower has five petals and ten stamens.

No-one knows why this plant is called herb robert. It may be named after Saint Robert of Salzburg, or be associated with the 'goblin' Robin Goodfellow, or with the garden robin.

## 25. Ramsons *Allium ursinum*

The inflorescence is an umbel (fig 1 f) and the six petals in each flower can be clearly seen. The plant belongs to the same family as the onion and the smell is unmistakable. The seeds are black.

## 26. Cow parsley or keck
*Anthriscus sylvestris*

This is a very common early-flowering hedgerow plant, with finely divided leaves. Each flower is about 3–4 mm in diameter. The whole inflorescence has

**25**

**26**

a slight smell of dung and attracts many insects which feed
on the exposed nectar.

## 27. Sweet cicely
*Myrrhis odorata*

The plant forms large clumps by
the roadside and is heavier looking than the cow parsley. It has
finely divided leaves of a lighter
green and rather creamy-
coloured flowers. When bruised,
the leaves have a distinct smell of
aniseed. This plant is visited by
many small flies and beetles
which crawl over the surface of
the flowers. The fruits are long
and brown.

**27**

**28**

**29**

**30**

### 28 & 29. Lords-and-ladies or cuckoo-pint *Arum maculatum*

This strange inflorescence is commonly seen by the roadside among the plants at the foot of the hedge. When the female flowers are ripe, the spadix (fig 7) produces a smell, disagreeable to us but attractive to small flies.

The flies make their way down through the spathe and clamber among the ripe female flowers at the base. They are trapped there by the sterile hairs. If the flies are carrying pollen, this may rub on to the stigmas. The stigmas wither almost at once and during the second night the stamens

ripen and shed their pollen on to the trapped insects. When this has been done, the sterile hairs wither, and the flies can escape. They may now carry the pollen to another spadix and bring about cross-pollination.

After pollination, the ovaries ripen, first into green and then bright orangey-red fruits which burst through the spathe. In Elizabethan times the thick tuberous root was used as a source of starch to stiffen the fine collars and ruffs worn then.

### 30. Comfrey
*Symphytum officinale*

This is a large hairy plant with coarse leaves. The flowers are usually purple, but some plants have white, yellowish or pink flowers. They are pollinated by bumble bees. Sometimes bees pierce the corolla tube with their proboscis and 'steal' the nectar without helping in pollination. The plant is still used in country districts as a poultice.

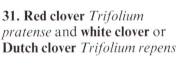

31

32

33

### 31. Red clover *Trifolium pratense* and **white clover** or **Dutch clover** *Trifolium repens*

Both these clovers can be found on roadside verges and waste ground. The red clover is usually in flower before the white, but as you can see here, they often flower together. Clovers are a valuable crop for feeding cattle and the seeds of a variety of red clover are sown with Italian rye grass for hay. The white clover spreads by growing long stems called runners. These grow along the surface of the ground and send down roots at intervals, anchoring the plant.

### 32. Great plantain
*Plantago major*

This plant needs little depth of soil and often grows close to the tarmac of the road and on ground where nothing else can grow. It is still sometimes called waybread, which shows its connection with the road or 'way'.

The rosettes of broad leaves and flowering spikes vary considerably in size depending on where the plant is growing. Sometimes those on dry paths are only 2·5 cm across, whereas on one spike in rich garden soil 474 fruits were counted.

### 33. Ribwort plantain
*Plantago lanceolata*

The flowers of this plant have distinctive drooping stamens. The tiny flowers at the bottom of the inflorescence open first and the stigmas ripen before the stamens. When the stigmas wither, the stamens emerge, shed their pollen and wither too. Other flowers further up the inflorescence then open and repeat the same process. The flowers are pollinated by the wind and may produce very many seeds.

**34**

**35**

**36**

### 34. Field poppy *Papaver rhoeas*

There are four native poppies but this is the commonest. It has four bright scarlet petals, often with a black blotch at the base of each. The fruit is globular and smooth. Poppies have no nectar, but beetles, flies and bumble bees and honey bees all visit the flowers for pollen.

### 35. Common mallow *Malva sylvestris*

This is the commonest mallow, but there is another species with small flowers (only 5 mm across) which can be found on waste ground. The French call the mallow *mauve*, and we use that word to describe the purplish-rose colour of the flowers. The roots of the related marsh mallow *Althaea hirsuta* are used in medicine and to make sweets.

### 36. Groundsel *Senecio vulgaris*

The brush-like yellow heads of the groundsel can be found almost anywhere. This is not surprising as the fruits are dispersed in several ways: they have a parachute of hairs and are easily blown away; they are sticky when moist, and stick to passing animals and people; and when eaten by sparrows they can grow unharmed from the bird's droppings. They can germinate at once and the time from seed to the formation of new fruits may be as short as five weeks.

### 37. Ragwort *Senecio jacobaea*

The bright golden yellow flower heads can be seen in summer in many places. They form almost flat-topped groups, much visited by various bees and flies. Each head bears about 70 disc florets and 12–15 petal-like ray florets. The leaves are attractive to the black and yellow caterpillars of the cinnabar moth, yet horses and cattle avoid the plant, for it can cause a fatal jaundice.

### 38. Oxford ragwort *Senecio squalidus*

The whole plant is less stiff than *Senecio jacobaea*. The flower heads are bright yellow, rather than golden, and have fewer ray florets. It is a native of Sicily and was first recorded on walls in this country in 1795. It is now spreading rapidly.

### 39. Creeping thistle *Cirsium arvense*

This is the commonest of the many thistles. It is the only one with lilac-coloured flower heads. These have either male florets or female florets, but not both. All the florets are tubular. The flower heads can have as many as 200 fruits. Each fruit has a long brown parachute of hairs.

37

38

39

41

## 40. Rosebay willowherb
*Chamaenerion angustifolium*

The leafy stems can reach 120 cm and the inflorescence is a dense raceme (fig 1b). The flowers are rose-purple in colour, 2–3 cm across, with two petals slightly larger than the other two. They are pollinated by insects which visit the flowers for nectar. The fruits are long and pod-like and contain large numbers of seeds.

## 41. Great hairy willowherb
*Epilobium hirsutum*

It is not so easy to recognise this plant as a willowherb. Its stems may grow to 150 cm and there are fewer flowers at the top. They are a similar purplish-rose colour to the rosebay, but the four petals are all equal in size and spaced equally. The flowers have eight stamens, four of which are longer than the others.

40

42

43

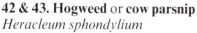

44

**42 & 43. Hogweed** or **cow parsnip**
*Heracleum sphondylium*

This is a stout strong-looking plant which grows up to 200 cm high. The stems are ridged on the outside and are often hollow. The inflorescence is an umbel (fig 1 g) made up of many smaller umbels. The flowers are all open at the same time. The outer petals of the flowers at the edge of each inflorescence are much enlarged (42) and the whole forms an almost flat table.

The flowers attract a great variety of insects, some of which spend a considerable time just resting and eating there. Most of the insect visitors come for pollen or nectar, but some wasps come to find their prey among the other insects. These wasps cause the insects to move to other inflorescences.

**44. Meadow cranesbill**
*Geranium pratense*

On the whole this plant prefers chalky ground, but it is common along many roadsides. The conspicuous violet-blue flowers attract bees which come for nectar. The fruits are long and sharply pointed. When the fruits are ripe they split explosively and curl up, scattering the seeds quite a long way.

45

46

47

48

**45. Lesser knapweed** or **hardheads** *Centaurea nigra*

You can often see the dark purple flower heads by the road-side in late summer. The flowering shoots may grow up to 100 cm tall and branch freely. The florets are usually all tubular disc florets with both stamens and pistils. Occasionally there is a row of ray florets round the edge which have no stamens or pistils. The flower heads are visited by many insects. The pale brown fruits sometimes have a few soft bristly hairs, but not enough to act as a parachute.

**46. Great burdock** *Arctium lappa*

It is possible to confuse this plant with the previous one, but it has huge leaves like rhubarb, and there are hooked bracts surrounding each flower head. The florets are all tubular and purple. They are visited by bees and butterflies. When the fruits are ripe the globular heads open wide to let them out. The hooks on each head cling to the coats of passing animals and so help in dispersal.

### 47. Daisy *Bellis perennis*

The name is a corruption of 'day's eye', because the flower heads are open in the day time and close up in the evening. Each short flower stalk has only one flower head with many narrow white or pink-tipped female ray florets and many bright yellow hermaphrodite disc florets.

### 48. Marguerite or ox-eye daisy
*Chrysanthemum leucanthemum*

The flower heads are very like those of the daisy, but much larger, 3–6 cm in diameter. The flower stalks may be from 20–70 cm long. Both ray and disc florets are fertile and one head can produce about 200 fruits.

### 49. Yarrow *Achillea millefolium*

The flowering period extends from about June right up to the end of the year. Sometimes the flower heads are pinkish, rather than white, but the plants all have a strong smell. The leaves are very finely divided and feathery. The flower heads are grouped together and look almost like umbels (fig 1f) but in fact they belong to the same family as the plants on the opposite page: each head is an inflorescence of tiny florets.

49

Usually each flower head has five ray florets surrounding up to twenty whitish tubular disc florets. They are attractive to a wide variety of insects.

Yarrow has been used in medicine from early times in an ointment to cure wounds, to prevent baldness and for toothache! It has also been used as a substitute for tobacco.

50

### 50. Foxglove *Digitalis purpurea*

Nobody could mistake this plant for anything else. The stem bears from 20–80 flowers with stalks arranged so that they all hang from one side. The corolla forms a long bell-like tube. It is purplish-pink on the outside and spotted and speckled inside. It is pollinated by bumble bees and produces large numbers of seeds.

People used to think that the fairies fitted foxglove bells to the paws of foxes so that they could move silently to catch their prey. And from the association of 'glove' and 'finger', or 'digit', came the name *Digitalis* in 1542.

The plant is an important source of digitalin, a valuable drug used in the treatment of heart disease.

**51**

**52**

**53**

### 51. Silverweed
*Potentilla anserina*

The leaves of silverweed are unmistakable for they are pinnate (page 50), with as many as twelve pairs of large leaflets alternating with smaller ones. The undersides of the leaves are all covered with shining silky hairs. The plant spreads rapidly over the surface of the ground by producing long stems called runners which root easily.

Single yellow flowers, about 1·5 cm across, grow from the axils of the leaves. They are attractive to the hoverflies which pollinate them. Each flower produces 12–50 dry fruits which are distributed in mud and by rain, as well as by birds.

### 52. Wood avens or herb bennet
*Geum urbanum*

This plant is in flower from April to October but is easy to miss. The branching stems reach from 30 to 60 cm and bear star-shaped yellow flowers. The fruits each retain part of the style which forms a hook. This hook catches on to the coat of passing animals and so helps in dispersal.

In medieval times it was considered to be a holy plant and was known as the blessed herb, hence its name herb bennet. It was supposed to be good for the chest, for pains and stitches in the side and for stomach disorders.

### 53. Birdsfoot trefoil
*Lotus corniculatus*

The yellow flowers are often tipped with red or orange so it is sometimes called bacon and eggs. The head of the narrow fruiting pods looks like a bird's foot and suggests its more common name. The plant is very common on open ground and is able to withstand trampling and grazing. It produces many slender stems running horizontally beneath the soil surface. These are capable of rooting to produce separate plants. The flowers are pollinated by wasps and bees which visit them for nectar.

54

55

56

### 54. White dead-nettle
*Lamium album*

This is a common plant. The upright stems bear pairs of nettle-like leaves with whorls of 3–10 creamy-white flowers in their axils. Each flower is nearly 2·5 cm long and the corolla has two lips; the upper lip forms a hood over the style and the four stamens, and the lower lip forms a landing platform for insects. The nectar lies at the bottom of the corolla tube. The flowers are pollinated by long-tongued bees.

### 55. Hedge woundwort
*Stachys sylvatica*

The square stems, the beetroot-coloured flowers and the strong smell all help to identify this plant. It grows up to a height of 100 cm, is often branched, and likes shady banks and waste places where there is fairly good soil. Whorls of about six flowers occur up the stem and form a terminal spike. They are pollinated by bees and each ovary can produce a fruit of four nutlets.

### 56. Toadflax *Linaria vulgaris*

This plant has a long flowering period in autumn. It seems to need little soil, for it is frequently found in very stony places. The flowers are two-lipped and can be opened only by quite strong bees. The nectar lies in a long spur at the base of the corolla tube. The plant spreads not only by its blackish seeds but by producing up to 100 shoots from its widespread lateral roots.

57

58

59

## 57. Bladder campion
*Silene vulgaris*

It is easy to recognise this common plant by its pale green bladder-like calyx which often has conspicuous veins. The flowers on one plant may all be either male or female or hermaphrodite. The hermaphrodite flowers are usually larger and are often strongly scented.

## 58. Ground ivy
*Glechoma hederacea*

The violet-blue flowers can be found from early spring onward, both by the roadside and on waste land. The leaves are not at all like those of the ivy.

It was said to cure a wide variety of ills, including stomach pains, ulcers, jaundice and gout, deafness and blindness.

## 59. Ground elder or goutweed
*Aegopodium podagraria*

This is the most widespread of the white umbellifers on waste ground. It can also become a nuisance as a garden weed. The underground stems spread and branch in all directions. One plant can spread to cover up to one square metre of ground in one year. The creamy-white flowers are produced in June.

### 60. Mugwort *Artemisia vulgaris*

This is another member of the Compositae family. It has many small compact flower heads. They grow on the branching flowering shoots which may be from 60–120 cm tall. Each flower head measures only 2–3 mm in diameter and consists of tiny marginal florets, all female, and a group of disc florets with stamens and pistils.

The flower heads are a dull yellow or purplish-brown, and are pollinated by wind. The leaves are dark green above but are covered with silvery hairs below. In the wind the whole plant looks greyish.

The related plant, wormwood *Artemisia absinthium*, is similar but has slightly larger flower heads and a stronger smell.

### 61. Sow thistle
*Sonchus oleraceus*

The flower heads are like small yellow dandelions, 2–2·5 cm in diameter. They are found on tall smooth stems which may be up to 150 cm tall. The leaves are dull bluish green, smooth and without spines. The florets making up the head are all yellow, but the outer ones may be tinged with purple below. They are visited by various insects, especially bees and hoverflies. They de-

**60**

velop into small ridged fruits, each with a parachute of silky white hairs which help in dispersal.

### 62. Scarlet pimpernel
*Anagallis arvensis*

On a bright sunny morning, the flowers are unmistakable. The plant itself is low-growing and has paired leaves. The stems are square in section. The slender

**61**

**62**

flower stalks each bear only one brilliant red flower from June to October. On warm sunny days they usually open at about 8 am and close again between 2 pm and 3 pm. They also close if the temperature falls and in damp and dull weather. This habit has given rise to the name poor man's weather-glass.

63

64

65

### 63. Knotgrass
*Polygonum aviculare*

This plant grows in many places, covering ground where nothing else grows. The wiry shoots spread in all directions over the surface and may extend to a radius of 60 cm. The 'knots' along the stem are the groups of tiny pink flowers, 1–6 in a group. These are self-pollinated.

### 64. Persicaria
*Polygonum persicaria*

This is a member of the same genus as the knotgrass, but is a stouter plant with straggly erect stems. The stems are often reddish in colour and the plant is sometimes locally called redleg or redshank. The leaves have a black patch on the upper surface. The pink flowers are borne in dense cylindrical spikes.

### 65. Curled dock *Rumex crispus* and Broad-leaved dock *Rumex obtusifolius*

These are the two most common species of dock and both are often found on waste land. In *Rumex crispus*, the edge of the leaves are very wavy (this is called 'crisped'), whereas in the broad-leaved dock they are not. The flowering shoots reach up to 90 cm and bear dense clusters of tiny greenish flowers. The flowers produce thousands of tiny fruits each year.

### 66. Chicory *Cichorium intybus*

This attractive plant is found in waste places and on roadsides where there is a certain amount of lime in the soil. The flower stems are stiff and roughly hairy. They vary from 30–120 cm in height. The bright blue flower-heads are 2·5–4 cm in diameter.

### 67. Stinking mayweed
*Anthemis cotula*

At first sight this plant resembles the marguerite but the leaves are much more finely divided, even feathery, and the whole plant has a sickly smell. As they age, the ray florets bend downwards. The plant is very similar to that of the scentless mayweed *Tripleurospermum inodorum* in which only the flowers are scented.

66

67

### 68. Rayless mayweed
*Matricaria matricarioides*

It is easy to overlook this very common waste land weed. The leaves are very finely divided, like the other mayweeds, and when crushed they smell of pineapple. There are no ray florets at all. The disc florets are a dull greenish colour. This is not a native plant and is thought to have come from Oregon, USA.

68

**69**

**70**

**71**

**69.** Here is a butterfly resting on a flower of meadow cranesbill. Very many of the flowers of verges and waste land provide food for insects. This may be in the form of nectar, a sugary solution produced by special glands in the flower, the nectaries. Or it may be pollen. In the meadow cranesbill, the nectar is hidden and can be reached only by insects with a long proboscis. It is more often visited by bees than butterflies.

**70.** Unfortunately some local highway authorities do not like plants other than grass to grow by the roadside. They sometimes use chemical sprays which destroy the vegetation altogether and mean that for a time nothing at all will grow in the soil. To some extent such drastic spraying has been replaced by selective weed-killers, which destroy everything but the grasses.

**71.** Many people became afraid that wild flowers would disappear. They complained against the destruction of the roadside plants by chemical sprays. Mechanical cutters are now used instead in many places. The photograph shows a verge where one 'swathe', or cut the width of the blade, has been made. This means that motorists can see the edge of the road quite clearly, but the rest of the roadside plants are allowed to grow naturally, to the delight of everyone who sees them.

# Hedges

Take a good look at a hedge and try to visit it several times in the year. First of all, find out the names of the main plants forming the hedge and then notice if they are ever cut. The farmer will call it a 'managed' hedge if every so often he cuts the tops of the new shoots, to stop upward growth and to encourage thickness by sideways branching, or if he intertwines the branches themselves to make a strong thick hedge. This 'management' also affects the plants which grow in the hedge. Black bryony, white bryony (11) and woody nightshade (8) are all more abundant in unmanaged hedges. Rose (4), honeysuckle (7), brambles (5) and goosegrass (14) are more abundant in hedges which are cut regularly. Look for differences on the two sides of the hedge and try to account for them.

Unfortunately, hedges between fields are often uprooted by arable farmers to make the fields larger. This helps with the economic use of big farm machinery. But hedges act as wind-breaks: once they are gone, the wind begins to blow away the top-soil in very dry weather.

Hedge plants too are an important source of food and shelter for many creatures. Brambles, elder (3) and ivy (9) provide cover for many birds' nests and their berries are eaten by thrushes and warblers. Many hundreds of insects can be found in a few metres of any hedge. Some of them feed on the leaves or obtain pollen and nectar from the flowers. Others find food and shelter in the leaf litter which collects at the base of the hedge.

*This is sandy soil blown on to the road by strong winds, in an area where hedges have been removed. It is obviously a danger to road traffic*

# Scramblers and climbers

Honeysuckle (7), the wild roses (4) and the brambles (5) are really scramblers. If there is no support available their arching stems will form untidy inter-twining masses around each other, or they will run along the ground.

Climbers are much more dependent upon other plants to enable them to rise above the ground and the stout branches and twigs of the hedge provide excellent support. The two bryonies are rooted in the hedge bottom and their shoots make their way up between the branches. The stems of the black bryony twist round the support until they emerge at the top of the hedge, whereas the white bryony produces tendrils which anchor it firmly. Without this help neither of these plants could survive for they are never found unsupported.

Goosegrass (14) and the purple tufted vetch *Vicia cracca* are frequently found among the stronger hedge plants. The tufted vetch will even make use of tall grasses to lift itself by means of its leaflet tendrils.

The 'host' plant does not usually suffer from the presence of the climbers, unless the climbers become very leafy. For instance, the leaves of the black bryony (10) and the larger bindweed (12) are very large, and where they grow thickly they can cast so much shade that the supporting plant cannot grow. This can be serious if it leads to gaps in a hedge.

*Traveller's joy using the other hedgerow plants for support*

# Serial flowering

As you walk along the lane or road in spring the first herbaceous flowers you see will be only a few centimetres tall. They will probably be the coltsfoot (15) or the lesser celandine (20). The yellow flowers are wide open to the sun and attract early flying insects. They will be followed by other low-growing plants like the primrose and the violet and the wild strawberry.

Then the daisies and buttercups appear, as well as wood anemones and speedwells, bluebells and ramsons (25), dandelion (18) and the clovers (31). All these are fully in bloom before the grasses grow taller and hide them from view. Their flowers must be pollinated before the taller plants develop.

Some roadside grasses grow very tall indeed, up to a metre or more. The later-flowering plants, such as the thistles (39), hogweed (42) and foxglove (50), must grow as tall or taller still to make sure that their flowers are fully exposed to the sunlight and to insects.

Waste places show a similar serial flowering, with the smaller plants in bloom first. Grasses are not such a problem at first, for they need some depth of soil to become well established, but the docks (65) and willowherbs (40 & 41) are tall plants which spread quickly.

*Late-flowering foxgloves are tall enough to rise above the tall grasses*

# Fruits and seeds

Plants produce flowers in order to produce seeds. The variations in colour, shape, scent and nectar are all means to this end.

Some plants, such as the hazel, have catkins which produce a large amount of dry pollen which is easily blown by the wind. Its female flowers have large sticky pistils which help to catch the pollen. Other plants have flowers which produce less pollen in fewer anthers. These have complicated mechanisms to ensure that the pollen reaches the stigma of another flower by means of insect visitors.

In general, cross-pollination, where pollen from one flower reaches the stigma of a flower on another plant of the same species, is an advantage. But there are some plants where the flowers are always self-pollinated, for example jack-by-the-hedge (21). There are others where the fruits are formed without pollination at all, such as the dandelion (18).

In almost all cases, once the pollen grains are on the stigma, each grain puts out a tube containing a male nucleus. This joins with the female nucleus in the ovule in the ovary; a process called fertilisation.

When the ovules in the ovary have been fertilised, they develop into seeds. The ovary itself becomes the fruit. As the ovary varies in different flowers (fig 5), the shape of the fruits varies too. The hawthorn and elder berries and rose 'hips' are familiar fruits. But the dandelion 'clock' formed from the head of florets, the long pod-like structures of the rosebay willowherb and the capsule of the poppy are all fruits too.

Sometimes such a fruit contains only one seed, as in the hawthorn and the dandelion, but it may contain a large number of seeds. It has been estimated that the rosebay willowherb may have between 300 and 500 seeds in one fruit and about 200 fruits on one stem. This means a total of at least 60 000 seeds from one shoot! A single poppy head may contain 1300 seeds, a toadflax plant 29 000 and a foxglove 75 000. A single dandelion plant may produce 2000 fruits in one season, a ragwort between 50 000 and 60 000 fruits and a large dock plant can produce 30 000 single-seeded fruits in one year.

Here are some examples of the many different ways plants disperse their fruits and seeds.

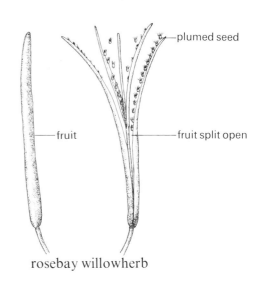

rosebay willowherb

*fig 8  Dispersal of fruits and seeds*

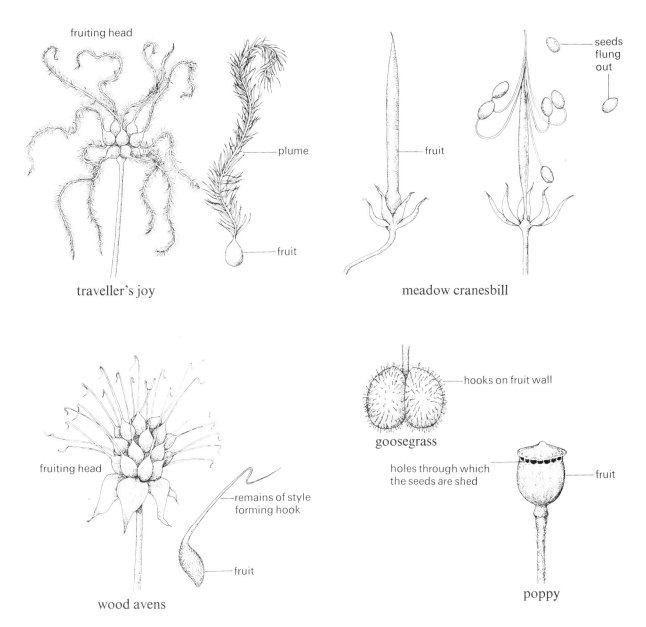

fruiting head

plume

fruit

traveller's joy

fruit

seeds flung out

fruit

meadow cranesbill

fruiting head

remains of style forming hook

fruit

wood avens

hooks on fruit wall

goosegrass

holes through which the seeds are shed

fruit

poppy

*fig 8  continued*

# Colonisation and competition

Fortunately, not all the seeds produced will survive. Some will not germinate at all and many which do will find conditions unsuitable for further growth and will wither away. But many seeds can rest in the soil for years and years before they begin to grow. This is called lying dormant. Half of the seeds of a dock which had remained dormant for fifty years grew successfully and quite a number after sixty years.

It is no wonder then that a variety of plants will establish themselves quickly on disturbed ground. The seeds may already be lying in the soil, needing only moisture and air in order to grow and produce complete plants. Lack of competition from bigger plants means that tiny seeds and small plants can establish themselves. Those which produce rosettes of leaves, like the daisy (47), dandelion (18) and great plantain (32), soon cover a considerable area of soil. Plumed and winged fruits and seeds are easily carried by wind. They lodge in tiny cracks in the rough ground, germinate and grow rapidly, so coltsfoot (15), groundsel (36), ragwort (37) and other members of this family are early colonisers. Those with underground stems and thick roots soon take a permanent hold.

When motorways are constructed, large areas of land are disturbed and it is interesting to see how the verges and the central reservation areas are colonised by plants. You can see the same plants for many kilometres on end. It seems likely that the fruits and seeds have been carried in the air currents set up by moving vehicles. The presence of so many members of the Compositae family in these areas seems to support this. Look at the motorways in your district and find out which are the plants you see most frequently. How did they get there? How do you think they spread?

*Rosebay willowherb has sprung up all over this neglected building site. In North America it is called fireweed, because it grows quickly after a forest fire*

# Herbicides

It is sometimes thought that hedges and verges are sources of weeds which find their way into fields of arable crops. This is a mistaken idea, for the weeds of cultivated land are almost all annuals which complete their cycle of seed → growth → flower → fruit → seed within a single year. Most of the hedge and verge plants are perennials with underground roots or stems which survive from year to year. They are unlikely to become established in fields where the soil is ploughed annually.

The spraying of hedges with herbicides right up to the hedge bottom does not destroy the plants permanently, but does make the vegetation less attractive. It may also reduce the shelter for small mammals and birds, and reduce the abundance and variety of insects and other invertebrates, some of which are very useful to the farmer and gardener.

The stinging nettle *Urtica dioica* is commonly found in hedges. It is generally considered to be an undesirable weed, though once it was valued as a vegetable and as a source of fibre for textiles. It is an important food plant for the caterpillars of several butterflies, including the tortoise-shell, red admiral, peacock and comma. It may be that it is the only food plant for as many as 27 different species of insect.

Herbicides do not kill the nettles completely. They destroy the above-ground parts, but the underground stems will produce new growth the following year. What they do kill are the creatures which depend totally on the leaves for their food.

*Stinging nettles*

# Verge cutting

In recent years some highway authorities have been using flail cutting machines on the roadside verges. These cut the vegetation very short, prevent the plants from falling over the roadway and improve visibility for the motorist. This is obviously necessary on busy roads and (71) is an example of good practice. Other authorities are not so thoughtful of the need to conserve our wild life, and cut right up to the hedge.

Repeated cutting throughout the summer is also unnecessary and destroys the verges as breeding places for plants and most especially for the butterflies. Some of the illustrations in this book show good examples of plants flowering well in the verges at the roadside but we must make sure that they are not destroyed by over-cutting.

Surprisingly, motorways may become the best conservation areas for many species. They are free from human interference, except from the maintenance staff, and the hard shoulder reduces the need for extensive grass cutting. Their verges may provide the safest places for much of our native plant and animal life.

*Grasses and flowers grow undisturbed on wide motorway verges*

*The roadside wildlife book*, Richard Mabey (David & Charles)
*Wild flowers of Britain and Northern Europe*, S. R. & M. Fitter and Blamey (Collins)
*The pocket encyclopaedia of wild flowers*, M. S. Christiansen (Blandford)
*Observers' book of wild flowers*, W. J. Stokoe (Warne)
*Wild flowers at a glance*, M. C. Carey and D. Fitchew (Dent)
*Oxford book of wild flowers*, S. Ary and M. Gregory (Oxford University Press)
*The concise British flora in colour*, W. Keble Martin (Ebury Press and Michael Joseph)

**Black's Picture Information Book Series**

| | | |
|---|---|---|
| 1. | Insects | Matthew Prior |
| 2. | Pond and marsh | James Whinray |
| 3. | Seashore | Ian Murray |
| 4. | Trees | Clare Williams |
| 5. | Conservation | James Whinray |
| 6. | Flowers and their visitors | Janet Davidson |
| 7. | Fungi | George Parkinson |
| 8. | Pests | Matthew Prior |
| 9. | Animals and plants in the fields | Valerie Duncan |
| 10. | Mountains, plains and rivers | Robert Webb |
| 11. | Prehistoric animals | David Seymour |
| 12. | What you can find in a park | Clare Williams |
| 13. | Mammals in Britain | Terry Jennings |
| 14. | Wild flowers of verges and waste land | Jean Imrie |

# Glossary

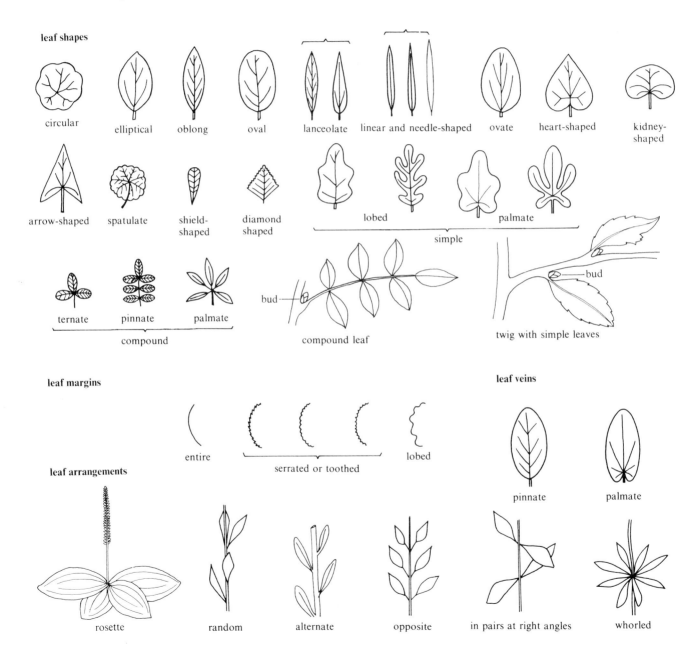

**leaf shapes**

circular  elliptical  oblong  oval  lanceolate  linear and needle-shaped  ovate  heart-shaped  kidney-shaped

arrow-shaped  spatulate  shield-shaped  diamond shaped  lobed  palmate  simple

ternate  pinnate  palmate  compound  bud  compound leaf  bud  twig with simple leaves

**leaf margins**

entire  serrated or toothed  lobed

**leaf veins**

pinnate  palmate

**leaf arrangements**

rosette  random  alternate  opposite  in pairs at right angles  whorled

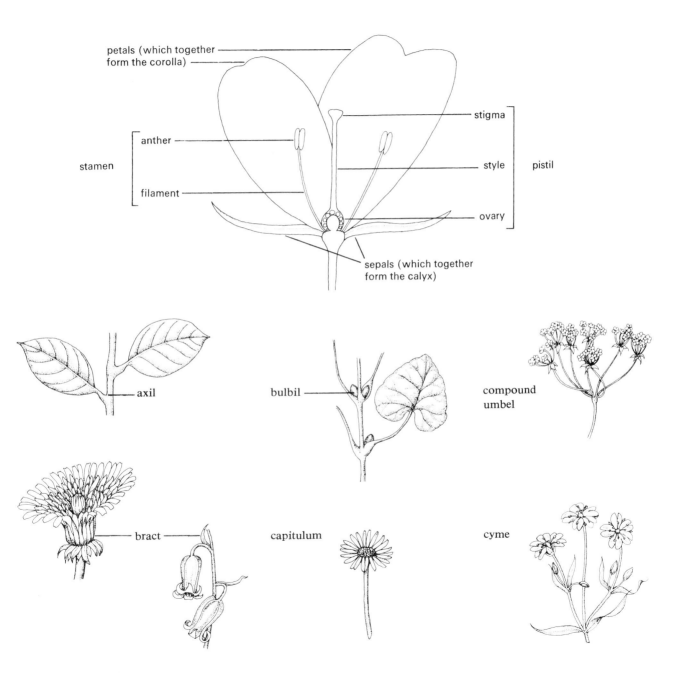

petals (which together form the corolla)

stamen

anther

filament

stigma

style

pistil

ovary

sepals (which together form the calyx)

axil

bulbil

compound umbel

bract

capitulum

cyme

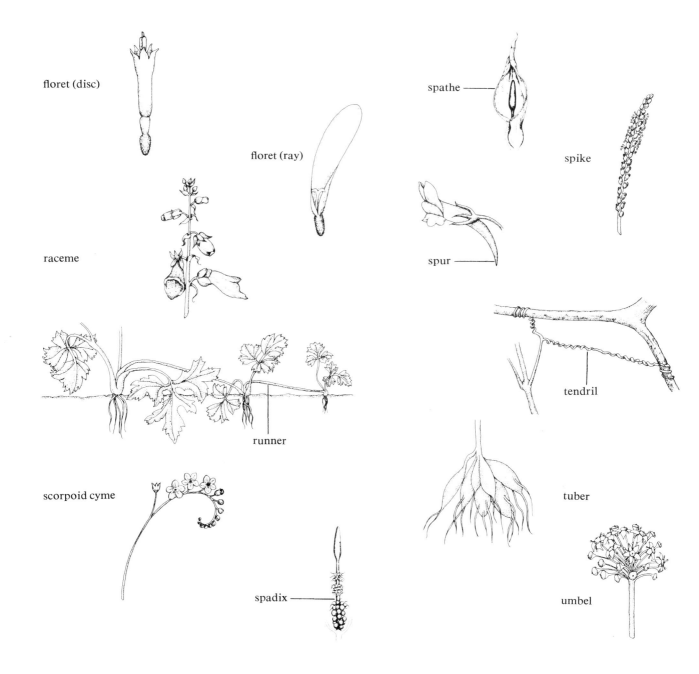

floret (disc)

floret (ray)

raceme

spathe

spike

spur

tendril

runner

scorpoid cyme

spadix

tuber

umbel

# Index of Latin names

# Index